P9-CMT-511

Read-About® Geography

New Hampshire

By Simone T. Ribke

Consultant
Jeanne Clidas, Ph.D.
National Reading Consultant
and
Professor of Reading, SUNY Brockport

Children's Press®
A Division of Scholastic Inc.
New York   Toronto   London   Auckland   Sydney
Mexico City   New Delhi   Hong Kong
Danbury, Connecticut

Designer: Herman Adler Design
Photo Researcher: Caroline Anderson
The photo on the cover shows a covered bridge and fall foliage.

Library of Congress Cataloging-in-Publication Data

Ribke, Simone T.
  New Hampshire / by Simone T. Ribke.
      p. cm. – (Rookie read–about geography)
Summary: A simple introduction to New Hampshire, focusing on its regions
and geographic features.
Includes index.
  ISBN 0-516-22742-4 (lib. bdg.)   0-516-27898-3 (pbk.)
1. New Hampshire–Juvenile literature. 2. New
Hampshire–Geography–Juvenile literature. [1. New Hampshire.] I.
Title. II. Series.
  F34.3.R53 2003
  974.2–dc21
                                        2003000370

CHILDREN'S PRESS, and ROOKIE READ–ABOUT®,
and associated logos are trademarks and or registered trademarks
of Scholastic Library Publishing. SCHOLASTIC and associated logos
are trademarks and or registered trademarks of Scholastic Inc.

1 2 3 4 5 6 7 8 9 10 R 12 11 10 09 08 07 06 05 04 03

Which state is called "the Granite State?"

New Hampshire!

Granite (GRAN-it) is a very hard kind of rock. It is under most of the land in New Hampshire.

Can you find New Hampshire on this map?

CANADA

WASHINGTON
OREGON
IDAHO
MONTANA
NORTH DAKOTA
MINNESOTA
WISCONSIN
MICHIGAN
NEW HAMPSHIRE
VERMONT
MAINE
NEW YORK
MASSACHUSETTS
RHODE ISLAND
CONNECTICUT
NEW JERSEY
DELAWARE
MARYLAND
Washington, D.C.
SOUTH DAKOTA
WYOMING
NEBRASKA
IOWA
OHIO
PENNSYLVANIA
WEST VIRGINIA
VIRGINIA
NEVADA
UTAH
COLORADO
KANSAS
ILLINOIS
INDIANA
MISSOURI
KENTUCKY
NORTH CAROLINA
CALIFORNIA
ARIZONA
NEW MEXICO
OKLAHOMA
ARKANSAS
TENNESSEE
SOUTH CAROLINA
TEXAS
MISSISSIPPI
ALABAMA
GEORGIA
LOUISIANA
FLORIDA

ALASKA   CANADA

MEXICO

HAWAII

North
West   East
South

5

The Old Man of the Mountain was made from red granite.

This pile of rocks stuck out of a cliff. In 2003, it fell.

In New Hampshire, there are mountains, the Coastal Lowlands, and the Eastern New England Upland. Much of New Hampshire is covered in trees.

The state bird is the
purple finch.

The White Mountains are in the north. The tallest mountain is Mount Washington.

There is snow at the peak even in the summer. The peak is the top of the mountain.

The Mount Washington
Cog Railway was the first
to climb to the top of the
mountain.

At the bottom, you can
visit the railway's museum.
At the top, have fun in
the state park or visit the
Sherman Adams
Observatory.

The railroad is over 100 years old!

Marsh

The Coastal Lowlands are made up of beaches, marshes, and meadows (MED-ohz).

Fishing is an important job in this area. Many people catch lobster.

The New England Upland
has hills, river valleys
(VAL-eez), and pretty
lakes.

Farms in this area grow
crops like apples and hay.

New Hampshire's largest
cities are Concord,
Manchester, and Nashua.

Concord is the state capital.

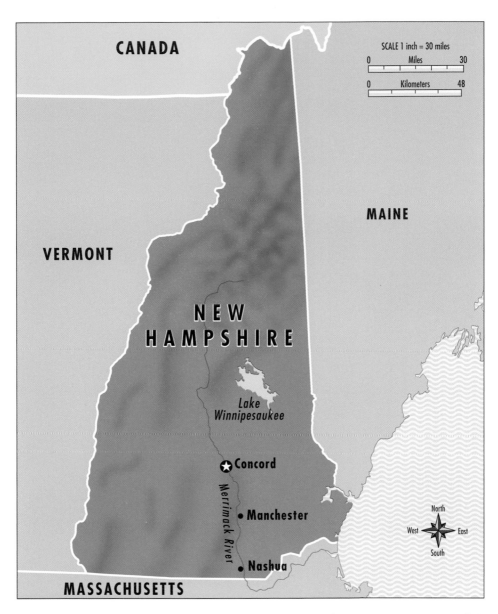

19

Many people in the cities work in hotels, stores, and factories (FAK-tuh-rees).

In some factories, people make computer chips.

Portsmouth is found along
the seacoast. Boats sail in
and out of its busy harbor.

This city played a part in the American Revolution (rev-uh-LOO-shuhn). Visitors can learn about it at an outdoor museum called Strawbery Banke.

The oldest school in New Hampshire is Dartmouth College. It was started in 1769.

25

Daniel Webster attended this school. He was born in New Hampshire in 1782.

Webster became a U.S. senator (SEN-i-tur). He was famous for his speeches.

Many people visit New
Hampshire every year.

It is a popular place to go on vacation. There is so much to see and do.

Words You Know

harbor

lake

lobster

marsh

Mount Washington

Old Man of the
Mountain

purple finch

31

Index

About the Author

Simone T. Ribke grew up on a horse farm in Maryland and now lives in New York City. She has a degree in education and writes children's books. Simone loves playing football and spending time with her cat.

Photo Credits

Photographs © 2003: Corbis Images/Dave G. Houser: 15, 30 bottom left; Dave G. Houser/HouserStock, Inc.: 3; Dembinsky Photo Assoc./John Gerlach: 9, 31 bottom right; ImageState: 25 (Andre Jenny), 16, 30 top right (Paul Thompson); Kindra Clineff: 23, 28; Photo Researchers, NY/George & Judy Manna: 8; PhotoDisc/Getty Images/Jim Arbogast: 20; Stock Boston: 3 (Margot Balboni), 26 (Chromosome), 14, 30 bottom right (William Johnson), 22, 30 top left (Peter Vandermark); Superstock, Inc./John W. Warden: 13; The Image Bank/Getty Images: 29 (Mike Brinson), cover (John & Lisa Merrill); The Image Works/Sean Cayton: 17; Visuals Unlimited: 11, 31 top (Warren Stone), 6, 31 bottom left (Roger Treadwell).

Maps by Bob Italiano